Testimonials

"Father Waters has gathered together articles written over the past 40 years reflecting on his experiences of dealing with couples preparing for marriage, couples experiencing prayerful families, couples struggling with marriage, laypersons evangelizing in ordinary ways, struggles of being a pastor in the modern world and the influence Pope Francis has had on his ministry. I find all of this that rare combination of both inspiring and useful!"

– Fr. James Martin, SJ,
author of *Learning to Pray: A Guide for Everyone*

"In this new collection of articles, Father William Waters, OSA offers a number of blessed insights into some of the recurring challenges priests encounter in pastoral ministry. His understanding of human nature and appreciation of the ordinary daily

struggles make his reflections real and realistic for both laity and priests. If you are looking for practical approaches, tinged with self-deprecating humor, for some of today's problems, I encourage you to pick up and enjoy these essays."

– Archbishop Alfred C. Hughes,
Archbishop Emeritus of New Orleans,
and co-author with Dcn. Larry Oney
of *A Gospel Path for Racial Healing*

"Marriage preparation, building projects, separately celebrating the seasons of Advent and Christmas in a society where celebrating Christmas usually begins immediately after Thanksgiving and ends before a new year begins, are among the many challenges that priests face in their ministries. Exploring these, and many other topics, the author shares the realities, as well as the frustrations, of being a priest and pastor today. People sometimes think that priests are knowledgeable about every aspect of their ministry. While Fr Waters admits: 'I do not pretend to have the answers, but I know some of the challenges,' he also has

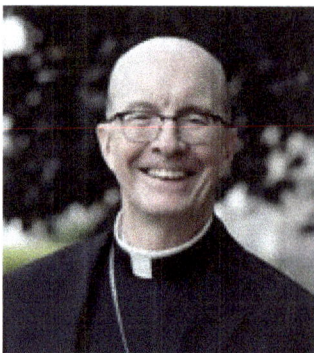

plenty of practical wisdom, acquired from serving over fifty-three years of ordained ministry, to convey to priests of all age groups. It is evident that Fr Waters understands priesthood with its many hats to wear. This book is a refreshing read and priests, particularly pastors, will readily identify with his experiences and benefit from his insights."

– Bishop Timothy Senior,
Bishop of Harrisburg

"This book is the revelation of a pastor's heart. Anyone who reads this work will be rewarded with both the wisdom of its author and the inspiration of his faithful witness. He is a priest who abides in fidelity to mercy, compassion, patience, and gentleness. May it come into the hands of many other priests."

– Dcn. James Keating, PhD, Professor,
Kenrick Glennon Seminary, St Louis, MO,
Director of Theological Formation,
The Institute of Priestly Formation

"When Fr Bill left our wedding reception, we told him not to change his process of helping engaged couples prepare for marriage. Under his guidance, completing our Marriage inventory forced us to ask the tough questions, ensuring we understood each other's values. Creating our Marriage Gameplan gave us the confidence to face any rough waters together, knowing we'd never abandon ship."

– Mark and Marisyl Alvino

Smelling Like the Sheep as We Minister to God's People

A compilation of articles on everything from
family spirituality to pre-marital sex to
the influence of Pope Francis

Fr. Bill Waters, OSA

Foreword by Dan Cellucci, CEO,
Catholic Leadership Institute

En Route Books and Media, LLC
Saint Louis, MO

⊕ENROUTE
Make the time

En Route Books and Media, LLC
5705 Rhodes Avenue
St. Louis, MO 63109

Contact us at **contactus@enroutebooksandmedia.com**

Cover Credit: Fr. Bill Waters, OSA
Copyright 2024 Fr. Bill Waters, OSA

ISBN-13: 979-8-88870-340-3
Library of Congress Control Number: 2025932371

Permission provided by *Our Sunday Visitor* and *National Catholic Reporter* for reprinting my articles, originally published in their pages.

Table of Contents

Foreword

I'll never forget the first time I encountered Fr. Bill. I had been in ministry for almost two decades, and I was helping with a project for my home Archdiocese of Philadelphia. I love the priesthood, and I have devoted my career to supporting their important role of leadership in the Church. That being said, I often wonder jokingly if the ontological change that comes with ordination renders a priest incapable of responding to email.

Not Fr. Bill. Not only was this Augustinian pastor responsive—he initiated! He wasn't satisfied with whatever the initiative's expectations were and thought there was a greater opportunity to engage the laity. He invited me to participate in the upcoming meeting of his parish's various councils on a Saturday morning. I accepted the invitation gratefully only to realize it also came with a preparatory Zoom session with some of his lay leadership prior. To spare everyone, myself especially, another Zoom, I offered to Fr. Bill that I did this type of thing all the time, and we would be fine without it. My host pushed back. "I want a good dialogue, so we need to be thoughtful."

That's been my experience of Fr. Bill Waters ever since. A priest, a shepherd, a man who is always thoughtful. He also always wants a good dialogue.

What you encounter in this shepherd is what you will encounter in these articles. Thoughtful and pragmatic prompts that encourage dialogue on a wide array of topics with stories and examples that not only help the reader understand, but more importantly, find their own opportunity for reflection. These essays feel like a pastoral visit with your longtime pastor—full of spiritual wisdom and guidance but never esoteric or out of reach, influenced by a lifetime of service to God's people and yet somehow personalized for each reader.

Despite the diversity of topics covered in this collection of articles, the theme that unites them all is the same belief that has defined Fr. Bill Waters' ministry as a priest for more than a half century – that ministry means service and that service is meant to help each individual realize how thoughtfully they are created by God, and to help them maximize that incredible potential in service to their Creator.

— Daniel J. Cellucci

Introduction

One of the absolute benefits of ministerial life in the Church is the opportunity to be so intimately involved at very significant times in the lives of the People of God. I believe Jesus very much had this in mind when he spoke of the loving care of the Good Shepherd. I also believe Pope Francis very much had this in mind in June 2021 when he said pastors should be "people capable of living, of laughing and crying with your people" and he urged priests to be "shepherds with the smell of the sheep."

I have been an Augustinian Friar for fifty-eight years and an ordained priest for fifty-three years. In those years I have been involved in a variety of ministries: thirty-eight years in parish life (thirty-four of them as a pastor in five parishes), four years as Vocation Director for our community, five years as a Formation Director, and six years in college campus ministry. Over the years, I also served as a police chaplain, Spiritual Director for Cursillo and most recently I have been involved in prison ministry.

During those years I had the opportunity to write eight articles reflecting my experiences and insights, mostly from the privilege of interacting with God's people, inspired by St. Augustine's attitude that for the people I am a priest but with them I am on the pilgrim journey to the Kingdom.

When I was Director of our Augustinian students studying theology, I participated in a program for Spiritual Directors at the Washington Theological Union directed by Tilden Edwards of the Shalem Prayer Institute. As part of that experience, I wrote a paper about spirituality in family life. It begins with the premise that family life is the domestic church. It is there that we have our first experience of God and the first instructions and models on how to develop this relationship. It was very inspiring for me to see the sincerity and creativity of so many families who incorporated spirituality into their family lives. Thus, the first article in 1981: *Spiritual Guidance in Family Settings.*

Although solid preparation for marriage is essential, after involvement with a number of engaged couples, I began to think that it would be more beneficial to talk with couples to help them make the decision if they should get engaged, rather than working with them after they were engaged. Thus, the second article in 1990: *Marriage Preparation Comes too Late.*

It is often said that if you want a marriage to work you have to work at the marriage. How may couples develop and strengthen their relationship? I found this an essential question as I encountered many couples struggling in their marriage. Thus, the third article in 1994: *Help Couples Avoid Divorce.*

Much has been said about evangelization in the Church. Pope Francis speaks about it regularly. Many people have a difficult time just with the word "evangelization" itself. For many, the concept of evangelizing is standing on the street corner talking about Jesus or knocking on doors selling bibles. We know when Jesus said to go into the whole world and proclaim the Good News, he meant to incorporate his teachings and our faith into the ordinary aspects of our lives. When I was pastor at St Augustine Parish in Philadelphia (the first foundation of the Augustinian community in the United States), we began each Parish Pastoral Council meeting with the members sharing how they "evangelized" in the previous month. Examples included sharing the parish bulletin with someone, saying "God Bless You" (rather than just

"Bless You."), telling someone they would pray for him or her, celebrating the anniversary of someone's baptism, inviting someone to a parish event, wearing a religious symbol, or sharing a positive religious experience with someone. Thus, the fourth article in 2016: *May He Soon Touch Your Ears to Receive His Word and Your Mouth to Proclaim His Faith.*

One of the things I dealt with in my thirty-four years as a pastor was the tension between the apostolic and administrative work of the pastor. I never felt I was ordained to organize capital campaigns, negotiate leases, or facilitate the restoration of buildings, but yet this is where most of my time was spent. Thus, the fifth article in 2018: *What the Bishop Didn't Say at Ordination.*

At the suggestion of one of our friars, Fr. Richard Nahman, OSA, I titled the compilation of these articles *Smelling Like the Sheep as We Minister to God's People,* in obvious *reference to Pope Francis. In all these articles there is an intimacy in relating to and caring for God's people. Throughout his papacy, Pope Francis calls us to do just that, but at times, he seems to be misunderstood. Thus, the sixth article in 2019: If*

Pope Francis is Confusing People, He is in Good Company.

In 2019, Father (now Bishop of Youngstown) David Bonnar, editor of *Priest Magazine,* asked me to write an article on how priests celebrated the Christmas season. In my mind, the answer depended on how priests celebrated the Advent season. Thus, the seventh article in 2024: *Christmas, a Holy Night, a Joyful Day, but is it a Glorious Season for Priests?*

One of the most satisfying, fulfilling and energizing things I do as a priest is helping couples prepare for marriage. The process in which I engage with the couples is a wonderful way to get to know them; as well as to influence their relationship, their marriage and their future family. An essential aspect of marriage, of course, is sexuality, which I believe is very misunderstood and misused in our society today. Thus, the eighth article in 2025: *Why Wait Till Marriage? It's so old-fashioned!*

In 2017, *the National Catholic Reporter* published an article on how Pope Francis influenced the parish where at the time I was serving as pastor. When I arrived at St. Augustine Parish in Philadelphia in 2014, I asked the Parish Pastoral Council if we could put all things "on hold" for several months and as a Council discuss Pope Francis' apostolic exhortation *Evangelii Gaudium* ("The Joy of the Gospel"). From those discussions we prepared a pastoral plan which we called "Creating a Community of Involvement and Evangelization." Thus, the ninth article: *Francis Effect Infuses St. Augustine in Philly.*

I am extremely *grateful to Dr. Sebastian Mahfood, OP for agreeing to have En Route Books and Media compile these articles into one book. It is my hope they may provide inspiration and ideas to those involved in the ministerial life of the Church on how to "smell like the sheep."*

I also would like to thank Dan Cellucci, CEO of Catholic Leadership Institute for writing the forward. I am grateful to Fr. Jim Martin, S.J., editor-at-large of *America Magazine*, Archbishop Alfred C. Hughes, Archbishop Emeritus of New Orleans, Bishop Timothy Senior, Bishop of Harrisburg, Deacon Jim Keating, Director of Theological Formation at the Institute of Priestly Formation and Mark and Marisyl Albino whose marriage I witnessed seven years and two children ago for all their kind words. As a group, they represent the Church: bishops, a religious priest, a deacon and laypersons.

A word of thanks also is extended to *Our Sunday Visitor* and *The National Catholic Reporter* for granting permission that the articles which originally appeared in their respective publications could be included in this book.

I am humbled that God has used me in my brokenness and sinfulness to be so intimately involved with the members of the Body of Christ. I am very appreciative of the lay people with whom I have collaborated and who have encouraged and affirmed me. I am grateful to my Augustinian brothers for their support and encouragement over the years, and in particular to the late Fr. Jim Wenzel, OSA, a close friend who preceded me in many of my assignments and who was a wonderful model of "Smelling Like the Sheep."

Fr. Bill
St. Thomas Monastery
Villanova University

Chapter 1

Spiritual Guidance in Family Settings

A common, underlying symptom of many problems which individuals have is a very poor self-image. People often have to prove that they are valuable and that they are worthwhile. Because of a negative self-concept, individuals often turn to drugs, alcohol and crime. Much sin is rooted in "trying to prove one's self" or in "trying to be God."

When one feels secure and loved, he does not have to find other means for gratification, acceptance or attention. As one grows in the realization that God is a loving Father, he grows in the realization that he is a child of God. God our Father loves us as much as He loves His own Son, Jesus Christ.[1]

If one really experiences that and comes to believe it, he can achieve a very healthy and a very positive self. image. Since I am a child of a totally loving Father, I must be special. I must be good. I must be all right.

---

[1] Peter G. VanBreemen, S.J., *As Bread that is Broken* Dennville, NJ: Dimension Books, 1974), p. 114.

As one experiences this realization, he will not have to prove that he is special, good or all right. This will have been experienced.

Everlasting Effect

An inevitable effect of a positive self-image is one's relationship with others. One who accepts oneself as he is will tend to accept others as they are. The individual will be better able to see others as sons and daughters of God and treat them accordingly.

As the person grows in the realization of the special relationship that exists with the Father, he will grow in the realization of the responsibility to respond to the Father's love. This response implies a more genuine and sincere attempt to live, to think, to act and to speak as Jesus himself did.

Spiritual guidance in the family setting can lead a young person to realize what a unique and special relationship he or she has as a child of a loving Father. This can have everlasting effects on how one looks at one's self, relates with others and responds to the gospel message in general.

When parents bring their child to be incorporated into the Catholic community, they are told: "You have asked to have your child baptized. In doing so, you are accepting the responsibility of training him (her) in the practice of the faith. It will be your duty to bring him (her) up to keep God's commandments as Christ taught us by loving God and our neighbor. They are then asked: "Do you clearly understand what you are undertaking?"[2]

As they answer "yes" to this question, they are beginning their journey of spiritual guidance, and they are agreeing to set the foundation so that in later years the child will be able to see how and where the Lord is working in his or her life.

If the parents do not live out this "Yes" which they publicly profess at the baptism celebration, they will end up with one confused child. They can send their child for more formal religious formation in the parochial school or in religious education classes for 20 years, but if they do not provide the spiritual guidance in the home, it will be much more difficult for

---

[2] *Rite of Baptism for Children* (New York, Catholic Book Publishing Co., 1970), p. 51.

the child to come to know and feel the love of the Father in his or her life.

Some children end up the innocent victims of parents who do not practice their faith but send their child to the parochial school or to an hour of religious education a week. The child is told how much God loves him; that God loves him so much He wants to be united with him in the Eucharist; that he is part of God's family and that God's family comes together to celebrate His love once a week.

The child is told all of these beautiful truths in one place while at home he might be verbally or non-verbally told something else. It is not far-fetched that the concept of God as a loving Father is never mentioned at home. It is not far-fetched that the family may never come together with the rest of God's family to celebrate His love. It certainly is not unheard of that the parents send the child off to Church while they themselves do not go.

The Beginning

In this atmosphere, children end up confused, and they rarely mature to be able "to reflect critically" on the Lord's working in and through their lives.

Kevin, Tricia, Mike, Paul, Greg and Brian Muldoon
Courtesy of the Muldoon Family

Kevin and Tricia are a young married couple from Massachusetts who have two small children. As they are in the beginning days of raising their children, they say: "We feel very strongly that most everything a child learns begins in the home. Children will form their ideas, beliefs and personality from the actions that they draw from their parents."

Vaune and Fred are from suburban Philadelphia. They have been married a short time and, as yet, do not have any children, but in looking to the future they say: "We feel that teaching by example is of great importance, especially in the eyes of the children. We believe it has a more everlasting effect on the children if they see their parents doing acts of love and showing kindness to their fellow man."

When can parents begin this spiritual guidance? They begin as they say "Yes" at the Baptism. At the Baptism itself they receive a candle and a certificate certifying that the Baptism took place. I often suggest to parents that they keep the candle and that they frame the certificate and hang it on the child's wall. I suggest that each year on the anniversary of the Baptism, they have a little cake in which they place the Baptism candle. They can have a little celebration with singing, a prayer of thanksgiving and, perhaps, if the child is old enough, a renewal of the baptismal promises.

If this were to take place each year, the child would begin to realize that his Baptism is important; he would begin to realize that as a child of God and a member of the community he is very, very important.

It is suggested that the Baptism certificate be hung on the wall as a constant reminder of what took place at the Baptism. As the child grows older and asks, "What is that?" it is a perfect opportunity for a parent to remind the child that he is a son of a loving Father and a member of a faith community.

As the child grows, he will prepare for other sacraments. It is crucial that this preparation be left not only to the school or to a religious education program.

As a child prepares to share the eucharistic meal with God's family, the parents can play a crucial role in letting the child know how important this is to them. If a parent communicates negative concepts about worshiping with the community, the child will incorporate some of these negative concepts into his own attitude. Some children regularly hear the following or similar comments: "I thought he would never stop preaching." "Do you realize that was five minutes longer than last week?" "I want to get the front parking spot so I can get out of there as quickly as I can."

These and similar responses do not help to provide a positive, constructive atmosphere for the child who is preparing to celebrate the Eucharist with God's family on a regular basis. As a child is preparing, however, there are ample opportunities for the parents to talk with him about what the Eucharist is, what the Mass means and what God's family is all about. There are a number of programs which have been prepared professionally to help parents in this regard.

When a child is preparing to celebrate the Sacrament of Reconciliation for the first time, parents can do a great deal to help.

First of all, if the child sees the parent taking advantage of the opportunity of experiencing the forgiveness of Christ, this can 'help tremendously to alleviate some fears which naturally may be present.

Secondly, it would be very difficult for a child to grasp the concept that God is forgiving his sins and selfishness if he has not experienced forgiveness from the parents. Again, parents can do a great deal in setting a very positive or a very negative tone.

Parental Influence

If a child never experiences forgiveness or is exposed to such statements as, "I think Confession is ridiculous; the Church should do away with it; it is one of the hardest things I have to do"; then the child will have a very difficult time appreciating how God works in his life in this beautiful Sacrament.

On the other hand, if the child is exposed to hearing that peace, joy, contentment and happiness result from experiencing the forgiveness of Jesus, he will be building a much better foundation to be able to see the Lord's forgiving and healing power in his life later on.

When an individual is preparing to receive the Sacrament of Confirmation, he is preparing to confirm what happened at Baptism. In doing so, one is assured of receiving the fullness of the Spirit's strength. The individual confirms that he wants to be a full member of the faith community. This can be mechanical, or it can have a great deal of meaning that will have its ramifications for the remainder of the individual's life.

The parents can have a great deal of influence on which of these two roads the preparation will take. If the individual senses that membership and participation in the faith community means very little to his parents, it probably will mean very little to the individual as well. The Sacrament can be very mechanical for one from this environment.

On the other hand, I have been involved with Confirmation programs where parents have been intimately involved in the preparation of their child. Some programs suggest that both parents and child read the same designated Scripture passage each week, reflect on it and come together at some time during the week to share their reflections.

Most Confirmation programs have some service projects incorporated into them to show the Christian responsibility that one has to others in the community. This takes on a more genuine meaning if the individual can see that his parents are involved in such activity on a regular basis. It then becomes another regular and normal way of living out daily the Christian life, not just another hurdle to be jumped before one can receive the Sacrament.

Marge and Jack are from Massachusetts and they are the parents of nine children, most of whom are now grown. It was important for them to have their children see that helping others is a regular and normal way of living the Christian life. "We tried to teach them to help each other by sharing, by doing for others; helping the elderly; doing errands for neighbors; visiting someone who is sick; but, mainly, doing these things and not expecting to be paid for them, to do them as an act of faith and charity. We feel they responded well to these acts because, even today, they are willing to help someone in need and do favors for people, without making a big deal over it."

Moving Experience

Using Scripture is a beautiful and excellent way for parents to be involved in spiritual guidance in their homes. I know of families who read the Sunday Scriptures together before they go to Church. When they come with the larger community to hear God's word proclaimed, they are not hearing it for the first time. Consequently, there is a deeper insight into the meaning of what the "Lord may be saying in those particular scriptural texts.

I know a family which, several nights a week, reads a very short scriptural passage at dinner. Several nights later they share how they were able to incorporate that passage into their lives. It is very moving to hear a high school football player say he spent an hour encouraging a dejected teammate who was cut from the team. This was how he integrated into his life the passage, "Whatever you do to the least of my brothers you do to Me."

One really sees Spiritual Guidance taking place when an eight-year-old girl says she gave half of her sandwich to a classmate who forgot his lunch because it was a way to imitate Jesus who multiplied the loaves and fishes for those who did not have any food.

Loretta and Andy from suburban Washington are the parents of 11 children. They have made great efforts to provide spiritual guidance for their family. In the area of Scripture, they relate that during Lent one year, each of the children took turns in picking a Scripture passage to explain to the family. "Maybe they were born hams, but they really enjoyed it. If the family really is a small Church or community, they should, at least on occasion, pray together:

"Our biggest problem is one of time. When to do it?" Andy thought it should be before dinner, but Loretta had some reservations about that. "Before dinner with all these teen-age boys is like feeding time at the zoo."

When one is deciding on a religious vocation, he is often involved in spiritual direction as he is trying to see where the Lord is calling him in life. This, generally, cannot take place if some form of spiritual guidance in this area has not taken place as the child is growing up. If the individual hears rather negative comments about priests, ministers, brothers and nuns, he probably never will consider the fact that this is a way of life to which the Lord may be calling him.

On the other hand, the foundation can be laid for the openness of such a possibility by positive spiritual guidance. If the parents have friends who are ministers or religious, they are affirming such a vocation. As a child grows up and is considering a number of options, parents can simply mention that the priesthood or religious life is one avenue he or she may not have thought about.

Again, they can lay the foundation for what may or may not take place in later years.

A good deal of the spiritual guidance which takes place in the family setting comes about as a result of spontaneous questions which are asked by children. This is true in many areas, but especially in the areas of death and sexuality. It is extremely important to respond to these and all questions sincerely, patiently and honestly, and in such a way that the child can see the Father as a loving Father who has a unique relationship with each of us.

As a child asks, "Where did I come from?" or "How come my body is different from hers?" or "Why is Mrs. McAndrews so fat?" – these are excellent opportunities to lay the groundwork for what later will be a healthy, Christian, sexual morality.

As a child grows up, it is inevitable that he or she will know or know of someone who dies. This situation naturally raises questions. "Why?" "Where did he go?" "If God is a loving God, why would he hurt Mr. Smith by taking Mrs. Smith?"

In answering such questions, we have a good opportunity to explain that God is not a puppeteer pulling strings. Maybe He allowed nature to take its course. Maybe He allowed these things to take place as a result of human error, selfishness, sin or whatever. Just as you cannot get blood from a stone because it does not exist within it, so, too, you cannot get evil from God who is all good. God does not want to see Mr. Smith or anyone else suffer. These realities are often the result of something else that comes about because of our human weakness.

Virginia Family

How these things are explained will vary with the age of the child, but they should always be explained in such a way that God is seen as the loving Father to whom each of us is integrally related.

As I have already suggested, if one has not experienced love, care, concern and forgiveness in the family setting, it is difficult to have faith in the love, care, concern and forgiveness of the Father.

It has frequently been said that one's concept of God is often strikingly similar to one's concept of his parents and, in particular, one's father. How to have a child experience these characteristics of the Father can and will vary from family to family.

I would like to relate how one family from Virginia does it.

Each Advent the members of this family pick the name of another member of the family for a "Pollyanna."

Let's say that Dan draws Rick's name, Rick draws Roger's name, Roger draws LuAnn's name and LuAnn draws Greg's name. During the entire season of Advent, Dan makes a special effort toward Rick, Rick makes a special effort toward Roger, Roger toward LuAnn and LuAnn toward Greg.

Until Christmas Eve, it is a secret who has whose name. At this time, the family gathers for what they call a "Reconciliation." Dan may go first. He tells the family how he has failed Rick and enumerates some of the ways he could have helped him but did not. He asks Rick for forgiveness. Rick verbalizes how he has broken his relationship with Roger and asks him for forgiveness. Roger tells the family he needs to ask forgiveness from LuAnn because of how he failed her. LuAnn, in turn, seeks reconciliation from Greg.

Sometimes, the session lasts for a good period of time. It almost always involves tears of joy and peace as the various family members experience forgiveness and the beauty of reconciliation from each other. Then they go to the next room where they exchange gifts, the bigger gifts being given to the one from whom they just experienced forgiveness and reconciliation.

Able to Relate

When you speak to this family about the love, care, concern and forgiveness of the Father, each member is able to relate to what you are saying because they have experienced it in the family setting.

Experiences such as these will set the foundation for the members of this family, as they grow older, to reflect critically on the Lord's love, care, concern and forgiveness for them as individuals.

When one enters spiritual direction, he is trying to obtain a better insight into how the Lord is working in his life.

In order to do this, it is essential that the individual be a person of prayer. One does not just become a person of prayer. A foundation must be set. Again, the guidance that can be obtained in the family setting is invaluable in setting this foundation.

We have already seen a few examples of what families can do in order to help a child become familiar with the Scriptures and how they can be incorporated into one's life. I would like to relate a few other examples of how the family setting can set the foundation for the individual to grow as a person of prayer.

Concerning family prayer, Loretta and Andy mentioned two things which they felt were helpful. In order to show the concern that they have for each other, the family would take turns at dinner stating an intention for which the whole family would pray. The second kind of family prayer they mentioned takes place on Christmas. The family prays together at the crib under the Christmas tree before they open their presents.

It was important for Marge and Jack to see to it that their children were familiar with prayer. "As parents, we started at a very early age to teach and show the 'Act of Faith.' Before a child talked, we would say morning and night prayers to him or her. They would learn by this and when they were old enough they naturally knelt to say their prayers when going to bed and getting up in the morning. Some nights for me it would have been just as easy to put the children right to bed but then they would say: 'Mom, you forgot to have us say our prayers' and they would get out of bed and kneel down to say their prayers.

"Another means of spiritual learning was grace before and after, meals."

One might ask if these things were effective for Marge and Jack. Marge answers by saying: "I can see that our children are giving their children a lot of the same direction that we started with them. So, they must have thought we had some good ideas."

Kevin and Tricia have two small children, Mike, who is two, and Paul, who is several months old. Kevin, who is Marge and Jack's son, relates that "It seems to us that Mike is starting to pick up a little of his religion – as much as a two-year old is able. He has always attended Mass with us and will now genuflect going into and leaving Church. We have started to have him say his prayers before going to bed. If we happen to forget, he will remind us. (This could be just to stay up longer since he is not too fond of going to bed!)"

There was a time when families said the Rosary together, had a May altar dedicated to Mary and attended the nine First Fridays together. Some may think it is sad that these things no longer take place. What is even sadder, however, is that in most families they have not been replaced by anything. I have heard of several innovative things which have been suggested for family prayer.

Once a week, perhaps, the family could make it a point to spend a half hour with each other in family prayer. They could go from person to person and have each member share what has been going on in his or her life. This could lead into a time for shared prayer when the members would be able to pray for each other.

A nice way for a family to watch the news is to take some time after it is over to pray for some of the people and some of the situations which were just seen. This helps all of us to remember that we are part of a larger family, God's family, and that we have a responsibility to each other.

Mimi and Terry from Miami, Florida, told me that on Holy Thursday, before going to the liturgy at the parish, they have a little prayer service in their home. In the context of prayer and Scripture they wash their children's feet. They explain to them that this is symbolic of their love and dedication to them.

Recently the children (teenagers) have asked if they might wash their parents' feet.

If the children of today are going to be men and women of prayer tomorrow, an important factor is the family setting in which they grow up. This family setting is the womb from which the children's prayer life and faith are nourished. It is in this setting that children are going to learn about a God in their midst who cares for them. It is in this setting that they are going to get the foundation to be prayerful persons who can enter spiritual direction to deepen a prayer life which has already begun.

Regular, Needed Role

Although parents have the primary responsibility for the spiritual guidance of their children and, consequently, for setting the foundation for spiritual direction, it would be a devastating mistake to indicate that they have the total responsibility. They need help in living out the "Yes" they professed at the Baptism of their child. The assistance they need can come from what is often called "The Extended Family."

Even at the baptismal ceremony, the godparents are asked: "Are you ready to help the parents of this child in their duty as Christian parents?"[3]

Other than giving presents at birthdays and Christmas, many godparents think their only other responsibility comes about if both parents die. The death of both parents is an extreme and extraordinary circumstance. In the normal course of events, godparents have a regular, normal and needed role to play. Their "Yes" is not to a question that asks if they would help if something drastic happened to the parents. Their "Yes" is saying that they will help the parents in raising the child as a Christian and, consequently, if they will help with the spiritual guidance of the child.

Parents need this help not only from godparents but from relatives, from the Boy Scout and Girl Scout

---

[3] *Ibid.*

leaders, from coaches and teachers. In general, we can say that the larger community has a function in the spiritual guidance of the child.

Vatican II recognized this when it said: "The task of imparting education belongs primarily to the family, but it requires the help of society as a whole."[4]

This is becoming truer and truer in our society where Christian families are finding themselves part of a subculture which is experiencing the competition and influence of a society whose values often run counter to the Christian values they are trying to communicate and live out as members of a Christian family.

Not Christian

Notice most of the advertisements on television. We are being brainwashed into believing that everything is supposed to be instantaneous, comfortable and convenient. It is suggested that if something is

---

[4] "Declaration on Christian Education," *The Documents of Vatican II*, Abbott and Gallaher, eds. (New York: American Press, 1966), p. 641.

not instantaneous, comfortable and convenient, then it is wrong.

This certainly is not the Christian message. I find it very difficult to see the connection between toothpaste or a car or a can of beer or a cigarette and sexuality. Many advertisements can leave you with the impression that whether you are married or not, if you are not in bed making love to someone, then there is something wrong with you. Most movies and many songs can leave you with the same message.

This certainly is not the Christian message either. As a result, many families which are trying to communicate Christian values, principles and morals to their children and, in turn, give spiritual guidance in their homes are finding themselves in competition with a world which is exposing their children to very different values, morals and principles.

Because of this, "The Extended Family" is essential to give support and continuity to the spiritual guidance which some families are trying to provide in the home.

As Loretta and Andy explain it: "Parents need support so that they feel normal. The kids need to be in contact with other kids whose parents have the same values so that they do not think that their own parents are weird. What has helped us in this regard is the involvement our kids have had in the teen club and sports programs provided by the parish. Parents can receive support from others involved in groups like the Christian Family Movement and Teams of Our Lady."

Several other couples informed me that Teams of Our Lady has been a great support to them. "Teams" is an organization made up of many small groups of four or five couples who meet monthly to give support to each other in living the Christian faith. These monthly meetings serve as a means to share some of the struggles and joys in living out the parental vocation.

Bill and Roberta from Maryland told me that "'Teams' has really made a difference with our family. It is our best example. The children really like the fact that we belong to 'Teams.' We include them a lot and try to make them see how you can really be happy picking good friends."

Chuck and Vivian belong to the same group as Bill and Roberta. They also feel that "Teams" gives them some of the support they need. "We joined

'Teams' seven years ago when our kids were nine and ten. Living in such a transient area and away from all relatives, we needed the support that 'Teams' offers. We needed to show our children that there were other families who loved God, had the same values and who did special things together like a family retreat. 'Teams' became our 'Extended Family.' This movement also gives our children the opportunity to know a priest as a person and not just as a name. This is a definite plus in this crowded area where there are 3,000 people in our parish.

"A few years ago, we had an argument over something trivial in front of our children. We were feeling the pressure of being involved in too many things. Finally, I said 'Let's quit Teams.' Well, our kids' ears perked up and they both shouted: 'No, please not Teams.' We were both pleasantly shocked at their dramatic plea. Needless to say, we stayed. We need that support. I think every family needs it. Some organization along these lines is just great."

Single-Parent Support

There are other groups akin to "Teams" that have similar goals. Cursillo, Marriage Encounter, Returno, Christian Family Movement, and the Charismatic Renewal are several other groups which provide support to parents who are attempting to live out their vocation and provide spiritual guidance for their children.

This concept of the "Extended Family" can be a very important support for single parent families. With the competition of our society's values, it is difficult enough for a home with two committed Christian parents to provide the necessary spiritual guidance. How much more difficult this must be for single parent families. With the number of separations and divorces constantly increasing, as well as the increasing number of unwed mothers keeping their children, the number of single-parent homes inevitably skyrockets. The Census Bureau reports that the number of families maintained by only one parent rose nearly 80 percent in the past decade.

At the time of the 1970 census, about 11 percent of all families with children still at home were maintained by one parent. By 1979, that proportion had increased to 19 percent – nearly one of every five families with children in the home.[5] The "Extended Family" or the larger community must become more aware of its responsibility for the spiritual guidance of the children of these families.

What is presumed throughout this article is a certain spiritual maturity on the part of parents. They are encouraged to participate in spiritual direction in order to help them as they strive to live a life of faith.

If parents do take this responsibility seriously, and sincerely seek ways to provide this foundation for their children, is there assurance that their children will grow to be spiritually mature men and women?

No, there is no foolproof assurance. Youngsters have free wills and can reject the values, needs and principles which parents may wish to pass on to them.

It also is recognized that young men and women, at times, need some space to stand back and question in order to incorporate and make their own some of these values.

---

[5] *The Philadelphia Inquirer*, August 18, 1980, p. 3, Col. 8.

Parents also must be balanced and use common sense in their approach. "You have to be cautious and know where to stop so that you do not turn them (the children) off," note Loretta and Andy. "Of course, we overdid things at times and the children kiddingly tell horror stories about some of the things we used to do."

If parents do not use common sense and if they are not balanced in their approach, they can do quite a bit of damage. Steve and Roanne, married less than a year, are aware of this danger. "We think the most negative approaches would be pressure, suppressing ideas, impatience and threats which we are sure, in moments of weakness, are hard to suppress. We plan to deal with spiritual guidance in our family on a daily basis using the events that happen to us in a positive way. We'll try the things we found effective when we were guided by our parents. For example, family meal blessings, holiday ceremonies, family get-togethers and consultations. Our hopes are that from our backgrounds, knowledge and experiences, we'll be able to guide our children spiritually into the faith we believe in and that has worked for us. From that we hope they'll be able to build the foundation and broaden their concepts as they enter the process of spiritual direction."

Special Relationship

Could a young man or woman grow into a spiritually mature person without growing up in the kind of environment spoken of in this article? Yes. Siblings who have grown up in the same environment have chosen different life-styles as well as different religious practices and beliefs.

Generally speaking, however, it seems to be true that if the care, sun, water and proper weather are present, the plant will grow. On the other hand, it is generally true that if these are not present, the plant will not grow.

The Lord has a very special relationship with each of us. As He worked through salvation history in the lives of Abraham, Moses, Jeremiah, Mary, Joseph, Peter, each of the saints, each of the popes, and others, so too does He want to work in and through each of us.

It takes real discernment, however, to be in touch with how the Lord is working in each of our lives.

This process is called spiritual direction – staying hungry for and growing in an awareness of God's elusive presence in our lives, directing our attention to God and His actions in our lives, totally surrendering ourselves to allow the Lord to work in our lives.

It takes a certain amount of spiritual maturity just to want to enter into such a process. If we are going to be honest about our relationship with the Lord, it is a process into which each of us should enter. Before we can enter into it, however, there is a good deal of groundwork that must take place.

This groundwork or foundation is what I have referred to as spiritual guidance.

It is in the family setting that this can most naturally and fruitfully take place. If this spiritual guidance takes place on a regular basis in the family setting, the children of such families have an excellent opportunity to mature to the point where they can enter the process of spiritual direction and see what a unique relationship exists with the Father and how the Father wants to work in their lives.

This chapter was first published as
"Spiritual Guidance in Family Settings"
in *The Priest* (March 1981)

Chapter 2

Marriage Preparation Comes Too Late

Harry and Loretta were engaged. Several months before they planned to proclaim very publicly that they "had come freely and without reservation to give themselves to each other in marriage," they came, as our diocese requires, to see me, their parish priest.

As I met with them, I did what I always do the first time I meet with a couple. I asked them how they would define, explain, or describe marriage. After Harry and Loretta spent some time talking about commitment, friendship, and sharing, I added a few thoughts of my own.

I talked about marriage being the total giving of oneself to the other in imitation of how Jesus gave himself totally and completely to us. I talked about the physical act of intercourse as the physical expression of that total giving. I explained that Jesus took on our flesh and became one with us, as do couples who take on each other's flesh and become one with each other. I further explained that the beauty and the risk of marriage lies in not knowing the future—in not knowing what the future will unfold after Harry says to Loretta and Loretta says to Harry, "I will be true to you in good times and in bad … all the days of my life." I went on to develop this with the usual examples from the worlds of finances, health, and children.

That was when Harry dropped the bomb. He said that if something happened to Loretta and she ended up in an irreversible coma, he felt he should be able to go on with another woman. He said he would not stop caring for Loretta, visiting her, or paying her bills, but he did not feel he should be without a companion for the rest of his life. He further felt that if there were young children and Loretta were in an irreversible coma, they should not be deprived of a mother as they grew up.

This created quite a discussion. Loretta did not think Harry really meant it the way it sounded. After all, none of us would know how we would respond to a situation until we were in it. In my thinking, there seemed to be a reservation in Harry's mind about giving himself totally and completely to Loretta. I began to wonder what I would be witnessing the day of the marriage.

I tested my reservations about Harry's reservations with some other priests. They had reservations about me. They felt the example of an irreversible coma was too extreme. Few individuals would know what he or she would do in a situation like that. The Archdiocesan Marriage Tribunal was more affirming. They felt I had very valid reasons to be concerned.

Strong Feelings

I met with another couple, Anne and Frank. Anne had her eyes opened wide when Frank said he would help with the physical care of the children when Anne was not home. But if both of them were in the house at the same time and a child needed to be fed, changed, bathed, or put to bed, then he would expect Anne to take care of the child because "it was the motherly thing to do."

While another couple, Helen and Allan, were going over the Preliminary Marriage Inventory (P.M.I.) with me, Allan let it be known how much it disturbed him that Helen had given such a high priority to exercise and physical fitness. He thought her commitment to this rivaled her commitment to him. This revelation on Allan's part opened up a lively, frank, and much needed discussion.

The second time I met with another couple, Ted and Judy, Judy said she felt Ted was "too busy for us to do enough things together." She felt this strongly because she thought Ted was purposely avoiding her. As our discussion evolved, Ted released some very strong feelings that had been building for a very long time. He felt pressured by Judy to live together. He felt pressured to become engaged. He felt pressured to get married. Anytime Ted tried to express his feelings, Judy would cry and scream. On one occasion, she had even threatened to harm herself physically by swallowing a bottle of pills. This really scared Ted. He felt guilty that he was the source of pain for Judy. As a result, he backed away from any confrontation.

As our discussion concluded, Judy and Ted agreed to live separately. They agreed to continue to see each other and to meet with me. They agreed to postpone their wedding, which was to have been celebrated in six months. Ted said he felt like a load had been removed from his shoulders. Judy said she felt like a failure and was embarrassed to have to tell others about this change. But she also felt better that everything was out in the open.

A Common Dilemma

Anyone involved in marriage preparation knows that the stories of these couples are not uncommon. And in each of the situations I have described, the revelations were not made until the wedding date had been set.

We all know how difficult, painful, embarrassing, and costly it can be to break an engagement and reverse marriage plans when arrangements have been made, announced, and paid for. To avoid such possibilities, even after painful revelations surface, the engaged man or woman will often resort to denial and familiar expressions, such as, "He doesn't mean that," or "She'll change after we're married," or 'This isn't that big of a problem." In the short term, the problem is avoided. But it is seldom gone for good.

I have come to believe that we, as church, would do a much better job of ministering to couples if we talked to them *earlier*, if we could help them with their decision to become *engaged*. How much more help we would be if we could change our approach and see them before the engagement is official, a ring is on the finger, and the video service has been ordered for the wedding!

An Impossible Dream?

Sounds great, doesn't it? The obvious problem is making it work. Routinely meeting with the couples before the engagement would call for a major change of thinking on the part of society, couples, families, priests, deacons, and pastoral ministers.

Bringing about this change is not, however, an impossible goal. Since Vatican II, the church has examined virtually every aspect of its life. We have changed the language and style of how we celebrate the eucharist and each of the sacraments—and these changes go far beyond a matter of words and rubrics. In parishes where the RCIA is well celebrated, for example, peoples' attitudes toward conversion, initiation, and adult faith commitment are evolving and deepening. At the same time, it is becoming increasingly rare to come across anyone who hasn't changed his or her perceptions and approach to what we now refer to as the Sacrament of Sick. And in many places people are beginning to realize that Mass is not something the ministers do and they watch, but something the ministers and they do together in the context of the primary ministry of the assembled People of God, the body of Christ. Attitudes and practices are shifting.

In the past generation we have seen the emergence—and acceptance by most Catholics—of eucharistic ministers, permanent deacons, married Episcopalian priests becoming married Roman Catholic priests, and non-ordained persons serving as parish administrators. Only a year ago, it was unheard of in our culture to have a non-ordained person be the official witness of marriage. And yet recently the U.S. bishops asked for and were granted permission from Rome for this to be possible in certain situations.

Changing Attitudes

We are already beginning to see a similar shift in attitudes and practice in our church's approach to marriage preparation. Rather than limiting it to a few months before the wedding, both Pope John Paul II and our conferences of bishops have begun urging us to see marriage preparation as "a gradual and prolonged process." In their 1989 publication: *Faithful to Each Other Forever: A Catholic Handbook of Pastoral Help for Marriage Preparation*, the U.S. bishops divided their marriage preparation material into four sections:

1) Remote Preparation (from early childhood),
2) Proximate Preparation (starting around the time of puberty),
3) Immediate Preparation (the weeks and months before the wedding), and
4) Pastoral Care After Marriage

Once we start thinking this way ourselves, once we start helping this idea of a gradual and prolonged process to catch on at the parish level, would it then be so difficult to change our practice and meet more often with couples *before* the official announcement of their engagement?

For the Good of All

The object here is not to invent new obstacles for couples, or to make them jump through more hoops to meet our program expectations, or to demand full-blown, mature faith commitments from them (after all, growing in love in a life-long journey). But when half of the marriages in this country end in divorce, and when a very large percentage of those who do stay together are not happy, something is drastically wrong. This reality certainly suggests that anything we can do earlier in the process to help couples communicate, spot problems, and grow in understanding and love would surely be for the good of all.

Such a shift in focus needs the support of our bishops' conferences, the individual bishops, and the personnel of the diocesan offices for family life. It also needs to be backed by the conviction and pastoral understanding of those of us entrusted with the hands-on parish responsibility of helping couples prepare for marriage. It would take a great deal of communication and commitment on the part of us all, and it will also take time. But we know that such change is possible, and I think we need it very badly.

If Only….

Harry and Loretta, the first couple I told you about, resolved their situation in a subsequent meeting. Harry said that if something happened to Loretta, such as an irreversible coma, he would not remarry while she was still alive, because Loretta would not want him to remarry.

Did Harry have the best motivations for saying he would remain married to Loretta "all the days of their lives"? I can't help thinking that if our conversation had taken place before there was an official engagement, Loretta would have gotten an insight into Harry she had not had before, and she would have been freer to decide not to marry Harry or at least to wait a while.

We will never know as long as we do the marriage preparation after the reception hall has been reserved, the cake has been ordered, the ushers and bridesmaids have been selected, and the deposit on the band has been paid.

This chapter was first published as
"Marriage Preparation Comes Too Late"
in *Today's Parish* (Nov. /Dec. 1990)

Chapter 3

Help Couples Avoid Divorce

Those of us working with couples are in a great position to remind them of some simple basics that are too often forgotten.

My path and the path of Ted and Alice, married for thirty-three years, crossed as they returned to Alice's home parish to prepare the funeral liturgy for Alice's mother. A few years before, they had come back to renew their marriage vows on their Silver Jubilee.

Drifting Apart

In the course of planning the funeral liturgy, I discovered almost accidentally that they had been separated for the last three years. Several weeks after the funeral, first Ted and then Alice came to see me separately. They were willing to put some time, effort, and hard work into reconciling a relationship that never should have been severed.

What happened? It was a classic case of what can happen when one doesn't work at a relationship. There was no malice, no abuse, not even a dislike for one another. Their relationship had disintegrated because they had become so caught up in their own, individual agendas.

What Ted and Alice experienced is extremely common. Statistics indicate that fifty percent of the marriages in our country end in divorce. Of the fifty percent that stay together, a high percentage really are not very happy. Many tolerate each other; they merely live in the same house. What has happened? Over and over again couples have not made the time or taken the effort to work at their relationship.

It often has been said that if you want a marriage to work, you have to work at the marriage. If you want the relationship to evolve, you have to work at the relationship. Neither a marriage nor a relationship just blossoms by itself without time and effort. A definite "game plan" is needed.

Those of us in parish ministry who work with couples are in a unique position to help them think through a "game plan" for their marriage. Some of the suggestions we might make to them include:

Solve differences quickly and maturely.

Do not go to bed mad at each other. We have heard that so often, but it merits repeating. St. Paul told the Ephesians, "The sun must not go down on your wrath; do not give the devil a change to work on you." When two people do not settle or bring closure to a disagreement, it snowballs. Imagination works overtime. "I'll say this. He'll say that." When two people have not settled an argument and it lingers, they cannot grow in trust or mutual respect.

Spend time with each other.

This may also sound obvious, but many couples get so caught up in business, work, children, finances, community affairs, and the like, that they do not spend much quality time with each other. Is it too much to ask that couples make it a point to spend one night a week together? As time goes on and their lives get hectic, the children know their parents will take them to basketball practice, cheerleading, dancing school six nights a week. One night a week they either do not go, or their friends' parents take them because mom and dad are enjoying their night together. Kids feel more secure when they know their parents enjoy each other, that they have a commitment to spend time with each other.

Vinnie and Ron have been best friends since grammar school. They are both married now. They were the best man in each other's wedding. They spend every Monday night with each other. They work on a car; they go bowling; they go Christmas shopping; they go to a movie. Every Monday night they do something together. This is called friendship. This is called commitment. This is called making time for a relationship to deepen. Are not husbands and wives supposed to be the best of friends? Would it not make sense to plan some quality time one night a week with each other? Based on the same premise, it would be a good plan for couples to commit themselves to going away together one weekend a year. When couples spend quality time with each other they eliminate the necessity of going to someone else to have their basic needs of belonging, affirmation, and acceptance fulfilled.

Some may respond that finances would prohibit them from spending one night a week or one weekend a year with each other. Some could also come up with some creative remedies: "We will watch the neighbors' children one night a week while they watch our children on a different night." A couple could suggest to their families and friends who may be giving Christmas, birthday, or anniversary presents that they give babysitting time or gift certificates. When something is important enough, we can usually find a way to accomplish it.

Pray with each other.

The 1980 United States Census reports that one in two marriages end in divorce. For couples who go to church regularly, the divorce rate is one in fifty. For couples who go to church weekly and read the Scriptures regularly, the divorce rate is one in 1,105. This makes sense. A Christian marriage is based on Christ. It is a sacrament because we make Jesus present in this union. We make him present by imitating him. How did Jesus love, forgive, affirm, and accept others? This is how I want to love, forgive, affirm, and accept you. Jesus becomes my model. I cannot imitate anyone whom I do not know. If a couple considers their union a Christian marriage, but they do not spend any time being with, listening to, and learning about Jesus, how can this Christian marriage endure? With fewer people going to church, reading the Scriptures, and praying, should we be surprised our divorce rate is so high?

On the same theme, would it be too much for couples to spend thirty seconds a day praying with each other? This may take the form of saying an Our Father or a Hail Mary out loud together. More adventurous couples might make up their own prayers. It is a beautiful sight to see couples spending a few moments over their child's bed at night and thanking God out loud for the child and for the gift of parenthood. There is some credence in the old slogan that families who pray together stay together. Marriage is the total giving of one's self to the other. Couples share their deepest secrets and wildest dreams. Couldn't part of the "game plan" be to share their prayer life with each other?

Renew the commitment on a regular basis.

Another married couple, Kevin and Maureen, shared with me that every several months they repeat their vows to each other. "I, Kevin, continue to take you, Maureen, to be my wife" and "I, Maureen, continue to take you, Kevin, to be my husband." "I promise to continue to be true to you in good times and in bad. I will continue to love you and honor you all the days of my life." They take off their rings and once again give them to each other: "Maureen… Kevin… continue to wear this ring as a sign of my love and fidelity. In the name of the Father and of the Son and of the Holy Spirit."

I certainly have been a part of many couples' fifth, tenth, twentieth, twenty-fifth, thirtieth, fortieth, and fiftieth wedding anniversaries where they have renewed their vows. Maureen and Kevin, however, opened my eyes to something new. This couple, married for four years, keeps the focus of their marriage as they verbally repeat their vows to each other every several months.

Too simple?

These four suggestions for a "game plan" may seem awfully simple, but sometimes the "awfully simple" really works wonders. Alcoholics Anonymous says its program is simple (not easy; simple): It is just a matter of one day at a time. Sometimes, we miss the obvious and the simple. Calvin Coolidge, former President of the United States, once said: "People criticize me for harping on the obvious…If all the folks in the United States would do the few simple things that they know they ought to do, most of our big problems would take care of themselves."

Jesus told us that a house built on sand will collapse when a wind comes; a house that is built on rock will survive a storm. The foundation of marriage is based on the very principles that need to be fortified and reinforced.

There probably would be fewer Teds and Alices in our world if we help couples prepare a "game plan" for what they will do as they work toward a happy marriage. Alice and Ted very likely would not be in the situation they are today if they had followed a "game plan." If couples are resolved to end differences maturely and swiftly, to spend quality time together, to pray together regularly, and to renew their commitment to each other often, there would be a strong foundation to withstand the winds and storms. Consequently, there would be fewer Teds and Alices working on reconciliations after thirty-three years of marriage.

This chapter was first published as
"Helping Couples Avoid Divorce"
in *Today's Parish* (April/May 1994)

Chapter 4

Ministry of the Laity:
Evangelization—Hearing the Word
and Keeping It

"May he soon touch your ears to receive his word,
and your mouth to proclaim his faith..."

According to CARA (The Center for Applied Research in the Apostolate) these words were said to the 713,302 babies in the United States who were baptized in 2013. Can you imagine what would happen if a high percentage of them really integrated this into their lives and really did "Hear the Word" and really did "Proclaim it"? In addition, during the same year in the United States there were 38,042 adults who were baptized and 66,413 adults who were received into full communion with the Catholic Church.

At a baptism each person is anointed, signifying that he or she shares in "The Priesthood of Jesus Christ".

I have heard it said, and I truly believe, that the crisis in the Church in the United States is not the lack of ordained priests, but the shortage of lay people who truly understand their priesthood. It is not just the bishops, priests and deacons who are "to hear the Word and to proclaim the faith".

Jake Kim, son of Sungben and Christina Kim, reacts at his baptism on 2/7/16 after he heard the words "May He Soon Touch Your Ears to Receive His Word and Your Mouth to Proclaim His Faith." Photo courtesy of the Kim Family

I am presently serving as Pastor of St Augustine Parish in Philadelphia, the first foundation of the Augustinians in the United States (1796). I have said to our parishioners that I am not in their workplaces where there are people who are wondering about God or wondering about the Catholic Church. I am not in their neighborhoods where there are people who are looking for peace, forgiveness, and acceptance. I am not at their family gatherings where someone shares a horrendous experience they had with the Church or shares a very bad misconception they have of the Church. I do not have the opportunities they have. People do not usually come to the parish office unless it is a requirement for a baptism, a marriage, an arrangement for a funeral, schedule a Mass or to seek a Mass Card or a certificate.

As much as Pope Francis has said that priests are to be among the people and "smell like the sheep", we do not have the same opportunities to evangelize as the ordinary lay person does.

After I arrived at St. Augustine Parish, I asked the Parish Pastoral Council if they would be willing to read and reflect on a chapter a month of Pope Francis' exhortation "The Joy of the Gospel". The plan is (we are still in the process) that after discussing five chapters in five months we will come up with a Pastoral Plan of evangelization for the parish, based on the words of Pope Francis and based on the realities of our parish.

Not knowing where the process would lead us and sensing my own impatience "to do something" I asked the Council if we could try a process in which we could be involved immediately. I asked them to get into small groups of three or four people. I gave them a list of eleven suggestions for evangelizing. (I have adjusted the list since.) I asked them to commit to do one of the suggestions in the next month. They then shared with the whole council how they would evangelize during the next month. One member, Steve, said it would be a sense of accountability to report back the following month, how they did.

When we think of evangelization, we often think of big projects. Or we think of being on street corners, holding signs and confronting people as they walk by. My point was to help them see that evangelization can be incorporated into the very ordinary events of life.

The suggestions were:

1) **BRING A PARISH BULLETIN TO SOME-ONE WHO DOES NOT NECESSARILY RECEIVE IT.** How often does someone say "I didn't know they had Masses at that time" or "I didn't know the parish had meetings for single parents, for young adults, for divorced and separated people, or a twelve step meeting"? Jesus met people in their own individual situations before He asked them to follow Him.

2) **INVITE SOMEONE TO MASS.** I know from being involved in Campus Ministry at Merrimack College in Massachusetts that students often would say "I would go to Mass if my friends did". I know I am not inclined to go to a movie by myself, but I am more likely to go if someone invited me. Some people may not have a way of getting to Mass, or for many reasons do not want to go alone. A friend of mine who was a student at St Michael's in Vermont was asked one Sunday evening where he was going when he left a dinner table in the cafeteria.

Ben said he was going to Mass. The next thing he knew his friends were in the pew next to him in the chapel. Ben didn't make a big thing about going to Mass, but neither was he ashamed or secretive about where he was going.

3) **INVITE SOMEONE TO A PARISH EVENT.** Some people may feel the roof would cave in if they entered a church building. After going to a Christmas concert or another event on the parish property, they may get a sense of friendship, welcome, and community. They may experience that they are not being judged. I know a woman who asked a co-worker one day if she wanted to go out for a drink after work. Patricia said "I am going to the opening of the parish mission at my parish tonight. Why don't you come with me? We can go out for a drink after that." The woman accepted Patricia's invitation and eventually enrolled in our RCIA (Rite of Christian Initiation of Adults) process.

4) **DISTRIBUTE FLYERS OF UPCOMING PARISH EVENTS.** Many college students major in marketing. Many people make their living by marketing cars, hair lotion, lottery tickets, vacation spots etc. How well does the church market itself? We certainly can use all forms of the media better. Flyers are just one way. Don't people look at them on bulletin boards, and elevators etc.?

5) **TELL SOMEONE ABOUT A GOOD CHURCH EXPERIENCE, LIKE A HOMILY OR CONFESSION.** How often do we incorporate into a casual conversation an experience we had at a ball game or the hair dressers? "You know I was at the mall yesterday and I saw Joe Smith and he said...." Can I be as comfortable saying in the midst of a normal conversation, not in a bragging way "When I was at Mass last week Father was talking about such in such in his homily"? Or "When I went to confession last month, I felt such a relief". Or "When I was coming out of church last week, I saw Bill and Peggy and

they were telling me about their children".
Can't we share, certainly not in an obnoxious
way, our religious experiences as well?

6) **TELL SOMEONE YOU WILL PRAY FOR
   THEM OR INVITE THEM TO PRAY
   WITH YOU.** I remember being asked to go
   to Children's Hospital in Boston one Sunday
   to baptize a baby who wasn't expected to live.
   The father, Jim, said to me that many people
   had said they would pray for them, but he
   didn't know what that meant. After we discussed prayer. I baptized the baby and asked
   if I could pray with them. They said they felt
   a sense of peace. I maintain they experienced
   the presence of God. Jesus said, "Where two
   or three gather in my name, there I am in the
   midst of them." This may not have happened
   if family and friends didn't say they would
   pray for them. If someone gives permission to
   pray with them, that prayer which is offered
   can be spontaneous or memorized and as
   short as fifteen seconds, but it sets a tone, an

environment and makes an impact. God's presence is felt.

7) **IF AWAY ON A WEEKEND WITH FAMILY OR FRIENDS MAKE IT A POINT TO GET TO MASS.** We are very familiar with the expression that actions speak louder than words. Recently at a family Christmas dinner, my niece's husband was showing me an "app" on his phone that no matter where Kevin is (he has three daughters in different colleges in Chicago, Philadelphia and Boston) he can see where and what time Mass is being celebrated nearby-- not unlike my GPS that can tell me where the closest McDonalds is. Imagine the impact it has, not in a holier than thou attitude, that others know the Eucharist is important for Kevin, even when on vacation or away from home.

8) **WEAR A RELIGIOUS SYMBOL, PIN OR CROSS, AND SEE THE CONVERSATION THAT CAN EVOLVE.** Recently I was in a "hot tub" and a woman asked me about the

medal around my neck. When I told her it was the seal of the Augustinian Order to which I belong, we got into a conversation about who the Augustinians are, who St. Augustine was, and how the different religious orders are distinct from each other. I answered the latter by letting her that the Augustinians were the best. Many people wear a symbol during the entire season of Lent. Isn't that what ashes on Ash Wednesday do? They signify that I am acknowledging that I am a sinner and I intend to repent. We never know what grace comes from outward signs.

9) **INFORM SOMEONE WHO'S MOVED INTO MY CONDO, APARTMENT, OR NEIGHBORHOOD ABOUT MY PARISH.** Jesus said, "I was a stranger and you welcomed me". As we help new neighbors get oriented (where the library is, where the delicatessen is) part of that orientation can be where the parish is. I can also inform the parish about new residents in the area and the parish may send a "welcome" letter.

10) **SAY GOD BLESS YOU WHEN SOMEONE SNEEZES**—even strangers. More often today if someone says anything at all when someone sneezes it is "Bless you", leaving the word "God" out of it, as God is left out of many situations in our society today. I have received many surprise but pleasant reactions at an airport or supermarket when I have said "God bless you" in response to a sneeze.

11) **ENCOURAGE SOMEONE YOU KNOW WHO HAS A QUESTION OR WHO HAS HAD A BAD EXPERIENCE WITH THE CHURCH TO COME AND TALK WITH SOMEONE WHO MAY BE ABLE TO HELP THEM.** Lay people are more likely than priests to hear the horror stories of other lay people. It may only take a little encouragement to have the person talk with someone who can answer the question or who can help the person work through the experience. More than once I have apologized to people who have received bad information (e.g. about annulments) or who have had a difficult experience with a priest (e.g. in con-

fession). Such clarifications and/or apologies have gone a long way. I recently witnessed the convalidation of a marriage of a couple who would fall into this category.

12) **CELEBRATE THE ANNIVERSARIES OF BAPTISM OF CHILDREN, GRANDCHILDREN AND GODCHILDREN.** We all celebrate our birthdays and the birthdays of friends and relatives. Most couples celebrate their wedding anniversary and many young couples celebrate the anniversary of their first date. Doing this signifies that they think these happenings in their life were important. What would the impact be if I placed the "The Baptism Candle" in a cake on the anniversary of my child's baptism and invited the godparents to dinner (and maybe the priest or deacon who baptized the person)? Or if there were some other recognition: a card, a phone call, a religious gift? Perhaps I could frame the Baptism Certificate and place it on the wall as I would a diploma, rather than putting it in the bottom drawer. Wouldn't this say some-

thing about the importance of sharing in the priesthood of Jesus? Does NOT recognizing this say something also?

These are all very simple suggestions (and there are certainly many more) for lay people to live their priesthood in very ordinary everyday circumstances.

Evangelization does not have to be doing missionary work in a far off country. As Pope Francis said in his interview with Father Antonio Spadaro, SJ. (*America Magazine*, September 30, 2013) shortly after being elected Pope, we need to be "able to do the little things of every day with a big heart open to God and to others". It is a lifestyle where we "hear the word and proclaim the faith" in the here and now in every day circumstances. If this were understood and integrated more into the lives of all the baptized, our Church would be drastically different.

This chapter was first published as
"Ministry of the Laity: Evangelization—
Hearing the Word and Keeping It"
in *The Priest* (July, 2016)

Chapter 5

What the Bishop Didn't Say
at Ordination

Role of the Pastor: The Tension Between Pastoral and Administrative

"Father, we need a new stove in the parish hall. The pilot won't work and we can't use the oven for anything."

"Father, we have evidence of termites and mice on the property."

"Father, the service man came to inspect the boiler, and he says we need a new boiler."

"Father, I just want you to know there are two broken windows on the top of the steeple of the church."

I have heard each of these statements and many others like them in the past several months. The latest and maybe the best was after a recent Sunday, 7:00 PM Mass. I was standing in the back of the church saying hello to parishioners and encouraging them to come to a beer and wine social in the hall with a tailgating theme in anticipation of the Eagles game in the upcoming super bowl. A little girl about 10 years old came up to me and said "Father, the toilet in one of the bathrooms is blocked." I wanted to say to her "and how was the homily?"

Bishop Daniel Turley, OSA, ordains three Augustinian Friars on June 26, 2021. Photo Courtesy of the Province of St. Thomas of Villanova.

I was ordained a priest on August 28, 1971 by Bishop Peter Van Diepen, OSA. To the best of my recollection Bishop Peter (as he told us on the morning of Ordination to call him) never said anything at the ordination about stoves, termites, mice, boilers, broken windows or anything about the overall facilities of buildings. He did talk about preparing well and preaching the Good News, celebrating sacraments prayerfully, encouraging others in the faith and reaching out to the poor and marginalized, etc. He did quote from the Gospel of St. Luke (4:18). "The Spirit of God is upon me; he has anointed me. He sent me to bring good news to the poor, and to heal the broken-hearted." He didn't say anything about fundraising or balancing budgets.

Not long ago I was at a Walgreens (at the corner of happy and healthy) waiting for a prescription. I was watching the pharmacist and thought he doesn't care if it snows tonight. He is not responsible to make sure the snow is removed and that customers have parking spots tomorrow. Shortly after that I was visiting a doctor whose office is attached to a hospital. It dawned on me that it was not his issue if the parking lot needed to be paved and sealed or that the temperature of his hospital was too cold or too hot.

I am presently serving as a pastor for the fifth time (St. Augustine in Lawrence, MA, St. Nicholas of Tolentine in Jamaica, NY, St. Mary of the Assumption in Lawrence, MA, Our Lady of Good Counsel in

Methuen-Lawrence, MA, and presently at St. Augustine in Philadelphia, PA). I certainly realized these issues of snow removal, parking lots, regulating temperatures in the parish buildings, etc. came with the turf of being a pastor. I am, however, becoming more convinced that there is something seriously wrong with this job description.

In the parish in which I am presently serving, I am the only priest assigned to the parish. I thank God every day I have other members of my Augustinian community who are very willing to help when needed, but understandably they are not responsible for the administrative side of the parish. I honestly do not know how pastors who live alone "do it." Our parish has a very competent Facilities Manager (a former lawyer, volunteer fireman, disc jockey, and owner of a handy-man business), but because of finances it only has been recently that this position is full time. I might add we celebrated our 220th anniversary as a parish last year and consequently our buildings are quite old.

In all of the parishes in which I have served, I had very competent and capable Facilities Managers. In each of the parishes I have had a very active Parish

Finance Commission. As someone who cannot change a flat tire or hammer a nail, I have depended tremendously on these men and women on the councils at each of the parishes over the 27 years I have been a pastor. As selfless as they have been in sharing their knowledge, experience and competencies, they are volunteers with a limited amount of time. The bottom line is the final responsibility and final decision about the boilers, roofs, budgets, etc. rest with the pastor.

Not only do the final decisions rest with the pastor, but this is where it is very easy to spend an incredible and inordinate amount of energy. Most of us probably spend more time on the administrative aspects of the parish than we do on the pastoral life of the parish. Not too long ago, someone said to me "That is why they call us 'Father' because a father takes care of the needs of his family and if the boiler needs to be fixed he takes care if it." I didn't respond but I thought "Yes, but if a father spends a disproportioned amount of time on the maintenance of the house, he will have a dysfunctional family."

I firmly believe something is wrong with our present system. Why can't we move in the direction of the pharmacist, doctor and other professionals who do spend some time on administrative duties but who at the same time spend the vast majority of their time and energy on their vocation?

The situation is actually getting worse. More and more we are having clusters and collaborative parishes where one pastor is responsible for two or three parishes. This means he is not only responsible for the pastoral life of several parishes, but he is also responsible for all of the facilities of each of the parishes.

Does this reality have an effect on vocations? As young men (or not so young) see how a great deal of the time and energy of a pastor is spent, is the ministry of priesthood so appealing? It is not only prospective vocations, but I have heard from more than one priest (including some Pastoral Associates) that they would never be a pastor.

What can we do? I do not pretend to have the answers but I know some of the challenges. I would like us to have some serious discussions about these challenges. How can parishes afford to hire competent people to be full time Facilities and Business Managers, giving them a decent salary to raise a family? Does canon law have to change so that the final decisions rest with the Business or Facilities Manager? If so, then in what way and how do we go about doing this?

In 52 lines Canons 528, 529, and 530 clearly describe the responsibilities of the pastor. These canons speak about the word of God being announced; the Christian faithful being instructed in the truths of the faith; providing catechetical formation; reaching out to those who have ceased practicing their religion; making sure the Eucharist is the center of the parish assembly; seeing to it that the sacraments are celebrated devoutly. It says in order to fulfill his office *in earnest* (my emphasis) the pastor should strive to come to know the faithful who have been entrusted to his care, visit families; make a special effort to work with the poor, the afflicted, the lonely, those exiled from their home land; support spouses and parents. The pastor is to promote the laity's proper participation in the Church; help the laity realize their connection with the (arch)diocese and the Universal Church. Functions which are especially **entrusted** (my emphasis) to the pastor are the celebration of the sacraments, assistance at marriages, imparting nuptial blessings, celebrating funerals, blessing the baptismal font during the Easter season, and imparting solemn blessings outside the church.

In 3 lines canon 532 says, "The pastor represents the parish in all juridical affairs in accord with the norm of law; he is to see to it that the goods of the parish are administered in accord with the norms of cannons 1281-1288." These canons refer to the administration of ecclesiastical goods, accurately collecting revenue, investing money, keeping well-ordered books, preparing reports, etc. It takes 52 lines for canon law to unpack the pastoral responsibilities of the pastor and 3 lines to unpack the administrative responsibilities. The lived experience is not the same proportion at all.

Does the pastor who is responsible for everything which canons 528, 529, and 530 outline also have to be the one who is responsible for what canon 532 outlines which in reality absorbs most of our time and energy?

When we seriously discuss these questions and attempt to respond to the challenges, maybe we can live as Pope Francis envisions our lives. He constantly encourages us to be among the people and to smell like the sheep. In his exhortation, *The Joy of the*

Gospel, he spends a great deal of time re-emphasizing what Vatican II said, that the primary role of the priest is to preach. "....priests, as co-workers with the bishops, have the primary duty of proclaiming the Gospel of God to all." (*Decree on the Ministry and Life of Priests*, 4 Chapter II, Section I). Pope Francis has urged us strongly over and over to go out and look for the ninety-nine lost sheep. I do not think he has ever said anything about our time and energy being spent on billboards, budgets (whether accrued or not), selling houses or building churches or elevators.

The present parish of which I am pastor (St Augustine, Philadelphia) is in the process of a three year capital campaign. This means an engineering assessment, a feasibility study, organizing a steering committee, task force committees and recruiters to solicit funds, writing a case statement, preparing a video, writing grants and especially asking individual people and corporations for large pledges. Of course, all of this has to be facilitated by someone. As much as I am spearheading and totally supporting this endeavor because of its necessity for the future of the parish and I have a great deal of competent help to do so, it still takes an incredible amount of my time, apprehension, and energy. I am certain Bishop Peter never said anything about this at ordination.

This chapter was first published as
"What the Bishop Never Told Us at Ordination"
in *The Priest* (June, 2018)

Chapter 6

If Pope Francis is Confusing People, He is in Good Company

I have heard it said many times from many people of different levels within the Church that Pope Francis confuses them. I would like to say that I believe he is in good company because Jesus Christ in his day confused many people.

Since Pope Francis was elected pope on March 13, 2013, he has not changed any Church teachings, doctrines, or anything in *The Catechism of the Catholic Church*. Very often when questions are asked about "hot button issues" such as abortion, homosexual marriages, contraception, and sexuality in general, he says very clearly he upholds the positions of the Church because "I am a son of the Church."

How is it then that people get confused? I think it happens because he realizes everything is not always clearly "black and white" and consequently he does not approach everything with rigidity. He continually talks about mercy and inclusiveness. That approach reminds me of Jesus.

Pope Francis

Jesus "hung out" with prostitutes and tax collectors. Jesus never said the things they did were right.

"As he sat down in his house (Matthew's) many tax collectors and sinners came and were sitting with him and his disciples. When the Pharisees saw this, they said to his disciples, 'why does he eat with tax collectors and sinners?' But when he heard this he said to them, 'those who are well have no need of a physician...go and learn what it means, I desire mercy, not sacrifice." (Matthew: 9:10-11) I am sure the Pharisees were confused.

I try to imagine the reaction of people when Jesus told the chief tax collector, Zacchaeus, that he was going to his house for dinner (Luke 19:1-6). I feel confident that their reaction was one of confusion.

In Luke (7:36-50) we read that Jesus went to the home of a Pharisee and as he took his place at the table, a woman, "who was a sinner," went to the house and anointed Jesus. He was criticized that he allowed her to touch him. Significantly, it was not just a small amount of oil as we use at baptisms, confirmations, ordinations and the sacrament of the sick. We are told it was an alabaster jar of ointment. John tells us that Jesus allowed Mary to anoint him with a pound of costly perfume made of pure nard that was worth three hundred denarii and could have been given to the poor. I understand that would be equivalent to about $6000 in American currency today. They had to be confused.

One of the most familiar stories in the Scriptures is Jesus not condemning the woman caught in adultery (John 8: 1-11). The scribes and Pharisees brought her to Jesus. It was legal to have her die by capital punishment, stoning. We do not know what Jesus wrote on the ground. It has been speculated he wrote the sins of the Pharisees and scribes who were present. They fled and Jesus told her, "to go and sin no more." I would love to have heard the conversation the scribes and Pharisees had when they gathered at the local watering hole that evening. They had to be confused.

It was the law not to pick heads of grain on the Sabbath. When the apostles did just that (Matthew 12:1-8), the Pharisees had to be confused when Jesus responded, "the Son of Man is lord of the Sabbath."

The Eucharist is central for us as a faith community. There is no Catholic Church without the Eucharist. It is the sign of our unity and bond of our community, the source and summit of our lives. When Jesus told his followers that there is no eternal life without eating his body and drinking his blood (John 6:35), they must have thought he was talking about cannibalism. Jesus never said to them that they were taking him too literally, nor did he reword what he said so that they would accept it. He repeated his statement three times. Many left him. They were obviously confused as they said, "Is this not Jesus, the son of Joseph whose father and mother we know?"

Jesus often broke the law concerning the Sabbath. It was on the Sabbath he cured the woman who was crippled for 18 years, bent over and was quite unable to stand up straight (Luke 13: 10-17). There had to be confusion when they criticized Jesus for curing on the Sabbath saying there were six other days for work to be done and he asked which one of them would not untie his donkey and give the donkey water on the Sabbath. It was on the Sabbath that Jesus cured the man with a withered hand (Mark 3: 1-6). They had to be confused when Jesus asked if it was lawful to do good or to do harm on the Sabbath, to save life or to kill. We are familiar with the man who was ill for 38 years (John 5: 1-18) and had no one to put him in the Bethesda pool when the water was stirring up and Jesus told him to pick up his mat and walk. John tells us the Jews wanted to kill him, not only because he was breaking the Sabbath, but he also was calling God his own father, thereby making himself equal to God. Jesus had them confused also.

When Jesus returned to Nazareth where he was brought up and spoke in the synagogue, "all spoke well of him and were amazed at the gracious words that came from his mouth" (Luke 4:22) and in a very few minutes they were filled with rage, got up, drove him out of the town, and led him to the brow of the hill, so they might hurl him off the cliff (Luke 4:29). It sounds to me as if Jesus confused them.

It seems obvious to me that after three years of public ministry people were confused when some thought he was John the Baptist, others Elijah and still others a prophet (Mark 8:23).

It doesn't take much imagination to know the people were confused as Jesus talked to them in parables: someone would go after one lost sheep?; a foreigner would help the man knocked off his horse and robbed?; a father would throw a party for the younger son upon his return after he squandered all his inheritance?; the rich man would go to hell while Lazarus would go to heaven? Sounds pretty confusing to me.

We know Jesus had to confuse people when he went against the culture of his day being accompanied by women (Luke 8: 1-3); committing an act of religious and civil disobedience when he cleansed the temple (Mark 11:15-19); spoke up for the poor (Luke 6:20; not demanding that the disciples follow the fasting regulations (Mark 2: 18-20); insisting that the children be allowed to come to him (Mark 10:13-16); and insisting that he act like a servant in washing the feet of his disciples (John 13: 1-17).

There are many other things Jesus said and did which caused confusion, but as St. John suggests at the end of his Gospel, too many to be included here. For example, "Do you think I have come to bring peace? No, I tell you, but rather division" (Luke 12:51). "Love your enemies, pray for those who persecute you" (Matthew 5:47). I would love to have heard the reactions to these statements and many others like them.

In many of these examples and others, Jesus went beyond the letter of the law. This is exactly what led to his crucifixion, speaking up for what he believed was right. He was following his conscience which the Church has traditionally said we have to do (*Cate-*

chism of the Catholic Church 1776-1794). We, however, have not always done a good job of guiding people on how to form a moral conscience. In his exhortation *Joy of Love* (37), Pope Francis says "we... find it hard to make room for the consciences of the faithful, who very often respond as best they can to the Gospel amid their limitations and are capable of carrying out their own discernment in complex situations. We have been called to form consciences, not to replace them."

Francis is quoted by John Allen, Jr. (*The Francis Miracle,* Time Books-2015) as saying "...rigid religiosity is disguised with doctrines that claim to give justification, but in reality deprive people of their freedom and do not allow them to grow as persons." Allen reminds us that at the end of the 2014 Synod of Bishops, Pope Francis said the Church must not succumb to a "hostile rigidity," a fussy legalism devoid of compassion and at the same time the Church must reject "a destructive do-goodism" and a "false mercy," a touchy-feely morality incapable of calling sin by its name. He went on to say the Church must not impose "impossible burdens" on people while not abandoning its core principles in order to win approval.

Consequently, with this mentality and with this approach, Pope Francis does not respond with rigid answers when asked about homosexuality ("Who am I to judge?"), and people in irregular marriages receiving Holy Communion, etc. and when he washes the feet of Muslims and women on Holy Thursday. If this confuses people, I say he is in good company, in the company of Jesus Christ.

This chapter was first published as
"If Pope Francis Confuses People, He is in Good Company"
in *The Priest* (March 2019)

Chapter 7

Christmas, a Holy Night, a Joyful Day, but is it a Glorious Season for Priests?

We had three Christmas Eve Masses and one Christmas morning Mass. Prior to Christmas, the combined choirs had a concert which is one of the highlights of the year in our parish, St. Augustine in Philadelphia. There also were innumerable parties. All the preparation and the actual decorating of the church and many other details, just like every other parish, had to be arranged. We had extra opportunities to celebrate the Sacrament of Reconciliation, namely after two of the Masses each Sunday of Advent. I needed to buy some Christmas presents that I gave to family and friends. (I don't send Christmas cards). I have a pile of thank you notes to write. It is Christmas afternoon, and I join family for Christmas dinner. I hear Christmas music (which I heard on the radio since Halloween) and even though as far as the Church is concerned, the Christmas season has just begun, I feel anything but in the Christmas spirit.

Hearing "O Holy Night," and "Joy to the World" just do not resonate.

Now it is the day after Christmas, and we are in the Christmas Octave. Is it a glorious season? I see the Christmas trees on the curbs waiting to be picked up by the sanitation workers and I am getting advertisements in the mail for Lenten ideas. I can't even hear Christmas music on the radio. They are getting ready for Valentine's Day. I want to scream "Please stop, I just want to enjoy Christmas. It just began."

This has been my experience in the past, but I have tried to change my approach to having a glorious Christmas season. What helps me to have the Christmas spirit, a glorious season, when I am exhausted and culturally Christmas is over? It may sound overly simplistic, but I try to have a good Advent. I try not to get "sucked in" to secular society saying the Christmas season begins at Thanksgiving and ends on Christmas Day. I try to take advantage of the spirituality of Advent.

This past Advent, my spiritual director suggested I reflect on "*The Coming of God*" by Sister Maria Boulding. It very much helped me stay in the "Advent Season" reflecting on how for many centuries the

Israelites were waiting and waiting. It helped me identify that my life is like the Israelites hoping and longing for the Second Coming of Jesus. My whole life is an Advent. It helped me reflect on how Mary was powerless and poor but faithfully waited, how the noisy world has little time to listen and wait and that I did not want to get caught up in that. It helped me to stay in the Advent season.

Of course, the spirituality of Advent is more than reading a book. In the midst of all the craziness, it is also keeping the basics going: reflecting on Advent readings, sharing scripture with others, getting to confession, etc. This all helps to set a tone of looking forward to celebrating Christmas and not looking forward to "Oh, thank God, that is over" which is how I would feel if I have been celebrating Christmas for the past four weeks or more.

Notice I did not say above "Christmas concert" or "Christmas parties" because I try to tell our parishioners we are not in the Christmas season until Christmas Eve. This is really counter cultural. So, we call them a Pre-Christmas concert and Pre-Christmas parties. I would love to wait (what Advent is all about) to have these things after December 25th, but that is really an uphill battle. Trying to make the distinction between a Christmas and a Pre-Christmas party may sound like semantics, but it sets a tone, at least in my head and I think it gives a message to others as well.

How about December 26th, how do I stay focused on the Christmas spirituality? I think first to acknowledge I am exhausted and find some downtime and not feel guilty about it. Jesus did that. "Jacob's well was there, and Jesus, tired as he was from the journey, sat down by the well. It was about noon." (John 4:6). Jesus told the apostles to take some downtime, "The apostles gathered around Jesus, and told him all that they had done and taught. He said to them, "Come away to a quiet place all by yourselves and rest a while." For many were coming and going, and they had no leisure even to eat." (Mark 6:30-31) Not to rest is counterproductive.

This past Christmas season, I made it a point after Christmas to make four "Christmas Visits" to some relatives and friends I have not seen for a while, some a two to three hour distance. This kept me in the Christmas spirit.

What helps me to keep the spirit of Christmas after December 25th? The answer for me is to not celebrate Christmas before December 25th. What helps me to have a glorious Christmas season, even when exhausted? It is to truly celebrate Advent.

This chapter was first published as
"Christmas, a Holy Night, a Joyful Day—
But is it a Glorious Season for Priests?"
in *The Priest* (December 2023).

Chapter 8

Why Wait 'Til Marriage?
It's so old-fashioned!

Spending time with young couples who are preparing to be married is a real privilege and a beautiful opportunity. It is no secret that the attendance of young people celebrating the Eucharist is low. It is also no secret that the vast majority of young couples preparing for marriage are living together—but not all, as I recently witnessed the marriage of a couple living in the same condominium building, but on different floors.

In the past I heard of priests who told cohabitating couples that in order for them to be married in the Church they would have to live apart for some time. Although I have never said that to a couple, I think that marriage preparation is a unique opportunity to talk with young people about the Church's teachings on sexuality. Too often people believe that the Church deems sexuality as dirty, bad, and sinful. This is a great opportunity to explain the Church's positive understanding of the beauty and the sanctity of sexuality.

Gene and Peg Gruner whose marriage I witnessed on August 13, 1977 and their daughter Susannah and her husband, Tim Kelley, whose marriage I witnessed on July 14, 2018.
Picture courtesy of Fr. Bill Waters, OSA

After our initial conversations when we get to know each other and I explain the marriage preparation process, I meet with the couple for what I call "the talk." We discuss what is marriage, what it means that it is a sacrament, and the place of sexuality in marriage.

We talk about marriage being the total giving of oneself, no matter what, forever. I use the analogy of their journey through married life being like a journey in a boat. No one knows the future, but as they are boarding that boat, they promise each other that, no matter what they experience on their journey, they will never leave the boat until they reach their destination. Similarly, on their journey in married life, they have no idea of their future in the areas like their health, finances, or children, but the commitment that they make is to give their whole selves to each other forever, no matter what they may encounter.

We talk about marriage as a sacrament because it reflects Jesus' total giving of himself to us, and that any sacrament is a sign of God's presence on our journey. Traditionally, we have said that the "couple" is the sacrament because they are the sign of Jesus in our midst, and there is nothing we can do to lose Jesus' love for us. We may not be aware of that love, and we may not appreciate it, but his love for us is not dependent on us, no matter what we say or do. When we imitate someone-maybe the way they laugh or walk-we are making that person present to another person and to ourselves. So also, when we imitate Jesus' commitment of total self-giving to us, we make Jesus present to ourselves and others.

We talk about sexuality in marriage. A couple expresses the commitment of "total giving" in the physical act of intercourse. They physically give their whole selves to each other, and they become one. They take on each other's flesh as Jesus took on our flesh. They become one with each other as Jesus became one with us. Traditionally, we have called this "consummating the marriage."

We know that if a couple exchanges vows, take beautiful pictures, enjoy a nice reception, but do not engage in sexual intercourse, there is no marriage. Put another way, they have made the commitment, but they have not "signed the check." In fact, it is grounds for an annulment. This is how beautiful the sanctity of sexuality is, and the positive light in which the Church views sexuality.

In order to stimulate some thought, reflection, and discussion, I pose a number of questions:

- I ask the couple if they were in a car accident that night and had to go to the hospital, could one of them give permission for the other one to receive medical care. They consistently answer "No." When I ask them why not, they respond "Because we are not married."

- I ask them if one of them may enroll in the other's health insurance. With few exceptions, they consistently answer "No." When I ask them why not, they respond "Because we are not married." (I usually then make a sarcastic remark about how old fashioned the hospitals and insurance companies must be if they will not allow them to act as if they are married if in fact they are not married.)

- I ask them if a politician is elected in November, can he or she make decisions the next day concerning the people they represent. They consistently answer "No." When I ask them why not, they respond "Because the politician has not yet been sworn in."

- I ask them if a person graduates from law school or medical school may that person act as a lawyer or a doctor without taking an oath. They consistently answer "No." When I ask them why not, they say because the person has not taken the oath. (I mention that this also applies to police officers, fire fighters, and other professionals.)

- I ask them if they are being married in May and I would not be ordained a priest or a deacon until August, would they allow me to witness their marriage. They always answer with a very strong "No." I ask why not and they respond, "Because you are not a priest."

When we discuss these questions, we always return to the one principle: why may couples act as if they are married if they are not "sworn in." That is, why may couples physically express the total giving of themselves if they have not actually made the commitment to totally give themselves, even though they have expressed their intentions to make the commitment both publicly and sacramentally. The typical response is "I never thought of it that way" or "I never heard it explained like that." I appreciate the opportunity to discuss these teachings and ideals, and the couples also seem to appreciate our discussions, which are always respectful and non-confrontational.

I understand that we live in a world of instant gratification, in a first-world country where all our needs are basically met; consequently, we want for little. We are not used to waiting for something that is appealing. With that in mind, I ask couples to consider the thought that, if they are sexually active on a regular basis, what is left to express their new relationship once they are married. If they are sexually active, I ask them to consider "abstaining" until they are married in order to have something to which to look forward and more conscientiously "consummate" the Sacrament.

I also give them ten "discussion questions" to continue the conversation on their own. I explain that unless they want to discuss it with me in the future, I will never ask them about their discussions including their decisions on sexuality. I believe I have done my part in providing them with the Church's teachings and ideals. I do, however, encourage all couples—no matter what their living situation might be—to celebrate the Sacrament of Reconciliation before the wedding.

I usually end our discussion by explaining to them that we live in a world that drastically needs to see and experience God's love. I also explain that, just as I am not an ordained priest for myself, they will not be a married couple just for themselves. Rather, they are desperately needed in our world to imitate God's love and to make God's presence manifested to us, reflecting God's covenant (commitment) with God's people.

After "The Talk," they take the Preliminary Marriage Inventory (PMI), and we discuss any statements with which they disagreed or were uncertain. I also ask them to prepare a "game plan" on what they will do to make sure the marriage survives. (See chapter 3 above entitled "Help Couples Avoid Divorce.") I ask them to dissect the vows that they will profess to each other on their wedding day: for example, Why am I taking you?; What do I mean by being true to you?; What do I mean by honoring you? Hopefully, this enables them to truly reflect upon and understand their vows, and simply not repeat the words that are presented to them at the wedding. Then we discuss the wedding liturgy itself.

I realize there is a tension between the real and the ideal. However, we need to raise and discuss the ideal, while being sensitive to the real. To be honest, I believe "Marriage Preparation Comes Too Late" as I explain above in chapter 2.

In the end, after this process (about 5-6 meetings, often on Zoom) some of which is delicate, they still invite me to the reception! More importantly—and almost without exception—couples preparing for marriage tell me how much they appreciate the process. Several positive ramifications of the process are that we are not strangers the day of the wedding and often we are friends in the days, in the months, and, sometimes, in the years that follow.

This chapter was first published as
"Why Wait 'Till Marriage? It Is So Old Fashion!"
in The Priest (January 2025)

Chapter 9

Looking for the Pope Francis Effect?

Francis effect infuses St. Augustine in Philly

For Augustinian Fr. Bill Waters, it's alive and well at St. Augustine Church in Old City Philadelphia.

A landmark near the Liberty Bell and Independence Hall, the church was founded in 1796 by the Augustinian Fathers, who also operate another venerable Philadelphia institution, Villanova University, located just outside the city limits.

St. Augustine is both a destination and a neighborhood church. Many come from outside the neighborhood to attend Mass, including a large community of Filipinos from the metro area who have adopted the church as their own. Center City Philadelphia has enjoyed a resurgence in recent years, as condos attract newcomers and retirees who return to city life after rearing families in the suburbs.

Upon taking on pastor duties in 2014, Waters sought a unifying theme for the eclectic parish and found it in the statements of Francis. He organized study groups around various papal documents before the pope visited Philadelphia in September 2015.

Waters discovered a renewed interest in things Catholic. Jews told him how much they admired Francis. And Catholics, he said, "feel good about being Catholic again."

St. Augustine began to feed off that new positive outlook by putting the pope's words into action.

"We built on what was already present in the context of what Pope Francis discussed about laypeople taking a more active role in the church," he told NCR. The parish calls its plan "Creating a Community of Involvement and Evangelization."

The Pastoral Council put aside all other business and devoted months to reading and reflecting upon the pope's apostolic exhortation *Evangelii Gaudium*

("The Joy of the Gospel"). After the study was completed, Waters challenged the group to come up with a pastoral plan to address the parish needs.

They looked on what was already in place and how St. Augustine could be a positive force.

Philadelphia's role as a medical hub generated increased parish interest in Gift of Life,[1] a program that provides hospitality to families and patients seeking transplants in the city.

Eight hospitals in the city perform transplants, and those procedures often involve long and lonely stays from those from out of town.

Some 30 parishioners are involved in providing meals and conversation to the families staying at a nearby Gift of Life facility.

"It gives us a sense of mission and purpose, doing something good for people in a difficult situation," said Rosemary Lorenz, a leader of the parish effort. Church volunteers shop and cook meals.

The parish took on the Francis challenge of evangelization with a conscious effort to reach out to young adults who have found a home in the City of Brotherly Love.

---

[1] http://www.giftoflifefamilyhouse.org/

The effort built on efforts already in place, including a 7 p.m. Sunday Mass, a spiritual bookend to the week for both old and young parishioners. It is the latest opportunity to attend Mass in the Philadelphia area and is similar to liturgy hours on college campuses. Noted for its music, the Mass concludes with a social.

Chesley Turner, a Villanova grad and parishioner for the past 10 years and Pastoral Council member, said the parish is cognizant of what Francis means by evangelization.

"People find they can connect to him even if they have a hard time connecting to the church as a whole," she said. "We wanted to tap into that."

That means connecting with young hipsters, a growing force in center Philadelphia.

The church keeps its doors open on First Fridays, a regular monthly program that encourages visits to art galleries and other attractions in the neighborhood. At St. Augustine, the doors are not only opened, the sounds of music emanating from the church regularly attracts a crowd at the monthly event.

Another outreach is via the 60 weddings that take place each year at the church. Couples often select the church for its classic architecture as well as the parish's reputation for welcoming.

Many of the couples are not churchgoers, but during the preparation process they are gently asked to consider coming to Mass at St. Augustine. Some take up the offer and become parishioners.

Ed Riehl, a native Philadelphian, came to St. Augustine after returning to the city four years ago. An attorney, he led a parish committee formed to implement "*Laudato Si', on Care for Our Common Home*," Francis' encyclical on the environment.

During Lent, parishioners were surveyed on whether they turned off their cars when they are idled and if they turned off lights in vacant rooms. Parishioners were then given tips on what they could do to improve environmental quality, such as shopping at markets that sell local produce. Parishioners volunteered for neighborhood cleanups.

"We feel we have parishioners who will want to get their hands dirty," said Riehl.

Another group formed around Francis' exhortation on family life, *Amoris Laetitia* ("The Joy of Love").

The group consisted of a married couple, a single woman, a divorced man, and another man in his second marriage. They reflected on the responsibility to form conscience and to help people prepare for marriage, and the various cultural and economic strains placed on contemporary marriage.

The group concluded with a day of reflection for married couples on Valentine's Day weekend. Eighteen couples, married from six months to 52 years, participated.

Bill Schmedding, another parishioner, said that the references to Francis, in various committees and regularly in homilies, reinforces the parish's mission and message.

"We are not cheering for the pope," he said. "We support him. It gives us some kind of direction and organization."

As a result, he said, there's always an opportunity and invitation for parishioners to get involved.

Waters noted that the parish activities, taken individually, are not unique to St. Augustine. Other parishes engage in similar projects. Yet taken as a whole, Francis has given parishioners an invitation to get involved, and the people of St. Augustine have responded, he said.

[Peter Feuerherd is a correspondent for NCR's Field Hospital series on parish life and is a professor of journalism at St. John's University, New York.]

This chapter, authored by Peter Feuerherd,
was first published as "Looking for the Pope Francis Effect?"
in the *National Catholic Reporter* (June 15, 2017).
Reprinted by permission of NCR Publishing Company –
www.NCROnline.org

About the Author

Fr. Bill Waters, OSA, was born in Philadelphia in 1943. After graduating from St. Anselm College in Manchester, New Hampshire he joined the Augustinian Community. After receiving a Master's Degree in Education (Villanova University, 1968) and a Master's Degree in Theology (Washington Theological Union, 1971) he was ordained a Roman Catholic Priest on August 28, 1971.

His first assignment was as Parochial Vicar at St. Augustine Parish in Lawrence, MA (1971-75). He then served as Vocation Director for the East Coast Augustinians (1975-79), and then Director of Students at Augustinian College in Washington., D.C. for the Augustinians who were preparing for Solemn Vows and/or Ordination. He returned to Lawrence as pastor of St. Augustine Parish (1984-93). He was the Vicar for the Lawrence Vicariate from 1991 to 1993. He then served as pastor of St. Nicholas of Tolentine Parish in Jamaica, New York (1993-97) and then pastor of St. Mary-Inmaculada Concepcion Parish in Lawrence (1997-2004). While pastor at St. Mary's, the parish in 2001 was named one of the 300 excellent parishes in the country by The Parish Congregation Study team led by Paul Wilkes. On August 6, 2004 Father Waters became pastor of Our Lady of Good Counsel Parish in Methuen and Lawrence, a position which he held until June of 2008 when he became a member of the Campus Ministry team at Merrimack College in North Andover, MA. In August of 2014 he became Pastor of St. Augustine Parish in Philadelphia, a position he held until July 1, 2024. He is presently residing at St. Thomas Monastery at Villanova University.

He served as a member of the Council of Priests of the Archdiocese of Philadelphia and as Chaplain for the Philadelphia Drug Enforcement Administration (DEA). Before he came to Philadelphia, he was a member of the Board of Directors of the Mary Immaculate Health Care Services, a member of Cardinal Sean O'Malley's Presbyteral Council in the Archdiocese of Boston, Chaplain of both the Ancient Order of Hibernians Division 8 and the Massachusetts State Chaplain for the Ancient Order of Hibernians. He was the former chaplain of the Lawrence Police Department, a past member of the Board of St. Anne Home in Methuen and a former member of the

Board of Trustees of the Lawrence Public Library. He was named Irishman of the Year in 2004 by the Hibernians and named the Grand Marshall of Lawrence's 2006 St. Patrick Day Parade. In October of 2012 he received "The Catholic Leadership Award" from his alma mater, St. Anselm College. In March of 2014 he received "The Cardinal Cushing Award from the Ancient Order of Hibernians.

He has authored the eight published articles that comprise this book.

www.ingramcontent.com/pod-product-compliance
Lightning Source LLC
Chambersburg PA
CBHW071819090426
42737CB00012B/2139